A Summary Hi
the Palazzo Dandolo

Anonymous

Alpha Editions

This edition published in 2024

ISBN : 9789364731027

Design and Setting By
Alpha Editions
www.alphaedis.com
Email - info@alphaedis.com

As per information held with us this book is in Public Domain.
This book is a reproduction of an important historical work. Alpha Editions uses the best technology to reproduce historical work in the same manner it was first published to preserve its original nature. Any marks or number seen are left intentionally to preserve its true form.

A SUMMARY HISTORY OF THE PALAZZO DANDOLO NOW ROYAL HOTEL DANIELI

VENICE
1896

VIEW OF THE EXTERIOR OF THE TWO PALACES WHICH FORM THE ROYAL HOTEL DANIELI

In 1805 the second floor of the Palazzo Dandolo, situated in the Calle delle Razze, and fronting on to the Riva degli Schiavoni, was bought by a certain Dal Niel, sur-named Danieli, from a member of the families of

Michiel and Bernardo, into whose hands it had come, partly by inheritance and partly by marriages. The new proprietor converted it into an hotel, giving it his own name—*Hotel Danieli*.

Although the use to which this Palace, which once occupied so large a place in the glories of the history of Venice, has been put during the present century is very different from that for which it was built, it has always been kept most worthily, first by Danieli, then by his daughter Alfonsina, the wife of Vespasiano Muzzarelli, then by his grand-daughter, Giuseppina Roux, and last by S.S. Genovesi and Campi; so that it had the honour, which it still possesses, of being chosen by Emperors, Kings, Princes, and Ambassadors, and by great men of all countries whose artistic travels bring them to this incomparable city, so justly called the « Pearl of the Adriatic ».

To the honour of the proprietors, who have succeeded one another in this hotel, be it said that although, from time to time, certain works have been executed in this historic Palace, to adapt it to its new use as an hotel, yet not only have the staircases, the saloons and the various apartments been preserved just as they were, but the artistic beauties, and the historical souvenirs, have been carefully respected; the stuccoes and frescoes of the XVIth and XVIIth century have been spared; and the portraits and heraldic shields of the Dandolos, the Bernardos, and the Mocenigos can still be admired today in their original positions.

PANORAMAS FROM THE BALCONIES OF THE PALAZZO
DANDOLO (NOW HOTEL ROYAL DANIELI)

PANORAMAS FROM THE BALCONIES OF THE PALAZZO
DANDOLO (NOW HOTEL ROYAL DANIELI)

It will surely be agreeable to the travellers who come to lodge in this remarkable building to know its origin and its history. We propose to give them a rapid sketch of both; and we believe it will not be uninteresting to them to know that in the halls and chambers they inhabit, some of the most important acts of the great Venetian Republic have been discussed and decided upon; and that in this Palace besides Doges and Senators, Kings and Ambassadors, Alfred de Musset (then a fair and charming young man in delicate health) took up his abode, in 1833, and Balzac, m.^{me} George Sand (who here wrote her novel *Leone Leoni*), and Victor Feuillet, who, for his magnificent romance « L'Honnêteté », drew his inspiration from Venetian subjects.

But to return to the ancient history of the Palace (now Hotel Royal Danieli) it was built in 1400, by one of the Dandolo families, but whether by that of the great Doge, Enrico Dandolo, is not quite certain. In the *Chronicles of Malipiero* which date from 1457 to 1500 we find the following passage « Today, the 28^h August 1498, have arrived the Ambassadors of Florence, Rucellai and Vespucci; who are lodged in the Palazzo Dandolo, in the Calle delle Razze ». We should here remark that the beautiful Gothic door, in the Calle delle Razze was originally the principle entrance, and the one on the Riva degli Schiavoni has only been opened in recent years for the convenience of travellers.

We find confirmation of what has been said as to the date of the Palace, and as to the family who built it, in the *Diary of Sanudo*, in which he tells us that « on the 7^h April 1498 the Prince of Salerno came to Venice. A most brilliant reception was given him, great *festas* were held in his honour, and he, and his suite of forty-four persons were lodged in the Dandolo Palace of the *Calle delle Razze* ».

Sanudo tells us again that « in 1499, this magnificent abode was prepared, by order of the Republic, to receive worthily the French Ambassadors ».

We could cite many other historical passages proving that this Palace had belonged to the Dandolo family, but one more, and a very interesting one, must suffice. In *Sanudo's Diary* we read again « On the evening of the 21 February 1531 the orator Cesareo, in the Palace Dandolo, Calle delle Razze, on the quay, gave a very great feast, with fireworks concerts, and illuminated boats, Spanish fashion, on the Canal of St. Mark's, on the occasion of the elevation of the king of Hungary and Boemia, to the dignity of a King of the Romans ».

This historic Palace passed from the Dandolos to the Gritti family, in 1536, by a deed of sale; and it is not without interest to note that to distinguish it from others of the same name, it is called in the deed, « that Palazzo Dandolo in which generally abides the Ambassadors of France ».

ATRIUM AND DUCAL STAIRS IN THE PALAZZO DANDOLO

After the Dandolos and the Grittis, the Michiel, the Mocenigo and the Bernardo families became its possessors by marriage, and they retained it till the beginning of the present century, when, as we have said, its second floor was sold, by the noble Dame Helen Michiel, widow of Alvise Bernardo to Dal Niel. Dal Niel left it to his daughter Alfonsina Muzzarelli, who was able, in 1840 to buy the first floor from the noble Filippo Nani, the heir of the Mocenigos; and thus the whole building passed to her daughter Giuseppina Roux, and forms the present Hotel Royal Danieli.

The interior of this beautiful Palace we have already described its architecture in Venetian Gothic, and Sansovino's hand is to be traced in many of its details. It well deserves the reputation that it enjoys of being one of the noblest hotels in the world—indeed its artistic beauties, and its historic associations, can only be equalled by its unique and romantic position. Mme Georges Sand, who lodged in the hotel in May 1834, as she watched from her balcony the sun setting over the enchanting scene spread out before her, writes in her Letters of a Traveller—« The sun had set behind the Euganean hills, great purple clouds hung in the sky over Venice. The tower of St Mark's, the domes of Sta Maria, and the forest of spires and minarets that rise from all parts of Venice, were drawn in black outline against the burnished horizon. The sky passed, by an admirable gradation, from cherry red to enamelled blue; and the water, calm and limpid as a glass, gave back the exact reflection of this immense iridescence. Nearer the town the lagoon was like a vast mirror of bronze. Never had I seen Venice so lovely and so fairy-like ».

To the beauty of a panorama unequalled in the world, that is spread before the windows of the hotel to its historic associations to the purity and the grandeur of its architecture, to the Venetian sumptuousness of its halls and chambers (including the green saloon of the Doges) to the magnificence of its Atrium and staircase—preserved in its original XV^h cent. condition, must now be added the important works of restoration and embellishment just completed by the present proprietors who by the aid of clever architects, artists and decorators, have studied the means of bringing into requisition all the modern appliances, in the way of Steam and Electricity, to produce luxury and comfort, without taking from this interesting Venetian monument its original character, which carries the traveller back to the epoch of the Dandolos, the Grittis, the Bernardos, the Michielis and the Mocenigos.

SCALA D'ORO

THE NEW YORK HERALD

(European Edition) of April 14th

says:

We have pleasure in offering to the readers of the NEW YORK HERALD a few details about this splendid hotel, which, because of its ancient history, its modern additions, its internal arrangements, its topografical position at Venice, is one of the most interesting hotels in Italy.

We will begin by pointing out the frame is worthy of the picture. Among all the cities of the world, incontestably the most beautiful and the most unique is Venice—the « Queen of the Adriatic ».

Venice for the traveler, for the artist, for the poet, is far more interesting than Naples, and even than Rome. The shores of Naples, however enchanting, the monuments of Rome, however incomparable, can be pictured by the imagination even without visiting them, but Venice can be comprehended and realized only by seeing it with the eyes and by living its life, and the more this is done, the greater becomes the admiration excited.

The enchanting mysteries of its canals and of its picturesque streets and calles, the grandeur of its monuments and of its palaces, which rise as by enchantment from the limpid water, the atmosphere of poetry and art which surrounds it, are not to be described, or if described present but a faint picture of the reality.

This, then, being the romantic frame, the picture as spread out before the windows of the Palazzo Dandolo, now Royal Hotel Danieli, which stands in the finest part of the Riva degli Schiavoni, is worthy of it, making an unequalled panorama, which extends from the Piazzetta with the Molo, the Columns, St. Mark's Church and the Doge's Palace away round to the Public Gardens. The front, which is due south, faces the broad Basin of St. Mark, dotted with gondolas and boats of all kinds, and the broad lagoons, with their treasures and their mysteries. The red church of San Giorgio Maggiore and the great dome of the Salute, reflect themselves in the water to the right, backed, in the far distance, by the blue volcanic hills of Padua: while to the left is Byron's island of San Lazzaro, and the long low banks of the Lido that defend Venice from the waves of the Adriatic.

SMOKING-ROOM AND AMERICAN BAR

PUBLIC DRAWING ROOM

But the palace itself, famous in the history of Venice, having been built in 1400 by the great family of Dandolo (and which is now the Royal Hotel Danieli), forms an integral part of the picture, for it is one of the most magnificent palaces of Venice; and we shall presently give our readers a historical sketch of it, which we trust will prove interesting. Meanwhile we must mention that to this ancient and sumptuous palace, with its Atrium and Loggia, with its grand ducal staircase, its ample reception halls, its « golden stairs », its rooms decorated with stucco and precious carvings, its Sansovino ceiling beams, its wooden mosaic floors, and its bifurcated windows and ogival balconies, which recall the history of Bianca Cappello, has been added a second palace, equally large and imposing, but one built on purpose for a hotel.

This second building is modern—modern in all its details, as we shall see in due course.

The exterior of these two palaces, of which the architecture presents a remarkable contrast, can be admired in the following engraving.

The building to the right of the spectator is the modern Palace, that on the left the ancient Dandolo Palace—each splendid in its own style—and the one in the distance is the famous Palace of the Doges.

To describe the interior of these two handsome edifices is very difficult, but the accompanying engraving, which represents the *Atrium* of the Palazzo Dandolo, with its magnificent ducal staircase, will give some idea of their beauty. Around this Atrium are a number of fine halls and offices, with the water-gate opening on to a side canal with a marble landing-stage for the gondolas. Near to the water-gate is the *Railway Office* (a convenience possessed by no other hotel in Venice), where tickets can be taken and luggage be registered without any trouble to the traveler. Next this is the luggage office.

Opposite the land entrance is the *Porter's Lodge*, where one or more porters are always to be found at the disposition of travelers. On the left hand is a *Post Office* with, for the greater security of all correspondence, a Government letter-box; and close by, the *Bureau of the Hotel*, with offices for the *cashier*, for *money changing*, and for *Bank business*.

Opposite the grand stairs is a luxurious *Smoking Room*, its walls hung with rich material, and furnished in Oriental comfort and style, with an *American Bar* leading out of it. Next it, are two spacious *Reading and Writing Rooms*, containing the principal newspapers and illustrated publications of the world.

READING ROOM

On the right hand of the main door is a large *Public Drawing Room*, style of 1700, with handsome stucco-work, and gilt furniture covered with rich stuffs, with the hangings and wall-coverings all *en suite*. This room alone would repay a visit to the hotel. Some idea can be formed of it from the following engravings, though, of course, the full effect of its richness and color is lost. In the two palaces there are a number of other such drawing-rooms, besides a concert hall, ballroom, music room and billiard room, &c. There are also bath rooms and douche baths on every floor. On the ground floor are the *kitchens*, the *wine cellars*, the *ice cellars*, the apparatus for *heating* the whole buildings by steam, thus spreading a uniform temperature throughout the two Palaces. Here is also the machinery for the *lifts*, the centre for the distribution of the *electric light* and the boilers and *syphons* for giving *hot water* direct into all the apartments. All this deserves being examined from the novelty of the systems employed and from the exquisite order and tidiness which everywhere reigns.

We will not describe the *bedrooms* and *sitting rooms*, except to say that they have all been recently done up and richly furnished with the utmost artistic taste and are all lit with electricity. Many of the apartments have been preserved in the original style, especially the *Saloon of the Doges*, No. 9, which with the adjoining rooms, Nos. 10, 11 and 12, all of which overlook the Riva degli Schiavoni and the magnificent panorama already described.

The *wines* and *the table* are a great speciality of the Hotel Royal Danieli, all being of the very highest order, and its *dining rooms* and *restaurant* arranged with small and separate tables, have an unusual character all their own.

The *dining rooms* are decorated in an entirely novel style and one that is truly poetic. The great windows of ground glass are transformed into eight lovely winter gardens of rare plants, which are reproduced in the big mirrors which line the walls, and the electric light, which hangs in delicate Venetian glass lily pendants round the ceiling, produces a most charming and unusual effect.

The two great *restaurant* halls are furnished in pure style of the Empire, for all the stuffs and decorations are copied from the best works that treat of that period, and are among the richest and choicest of that famous epoch.

Thus, by a series of ingenious combinations these two palaces, so different from each other in many ways, blend themselves in one harmonious and artistic whole, and in them are united the greatest luxury with the utmost comfort.

SALON OF THE DOGES

To give an idea of the whole we will imagine that a traveler is staying in the apartment of the Doge—which recalls all the pomp and grandeur of old Venice—to go to the breakfast-room and restaurant we will pass through the great Sansovino ball-room, then through the Rose saloon, by the side of which is the music-room (style Empire), and the gallery of tapestry and majolica, and thus reaches the Empire decorated restaurants which we have already described.

In the evening at dinner-time the traveler would, instead, descend by successive steps, through a Renaissance vestibule, to the beautiful winter garden dining-halls, which, especially when lit up by the soft radiance of the electric lilies, makes a perfect fairy scene.

Round the ball-room on the first floor runs an uncovered *loggia*, from whence one can look down into the court of honor, or Venetian Atrium, in which of an evening characteristic concerts are frequently given. From the first floor the great « scala d'oro » conducts one to the second floor, where are the spacious concert-room and various handsome suites of ancient and modern apartments.

To the honor of the proprietors who have succeeded one another, be it said, that although from time to time certain works have been executed in this historic palace to adapt it to its new use as a hotel, yet not only have the staircases, the saloons and the various apartments been preserved just as they were, but the artistic beauties and the historic souvenirs have been carefully respected, the stuccoes and frescoes of the sixteenth and seventeenth century have been spared, and the portraits and heraldic shields of the Dandolos, the Bernardos and the Mocenigos can still be admired to-day in their original positions.

Although the use to which this Palace, which once occupied so large a place in the glories of the history of Venice, has been put during the present century is very different from that which it was built, it has always been kept most worthily, first by Danieli, then by his daughter Alfonsina, the wife of Vespasiano Muzzarelli; then by his granddaughter, Giuseppina Roux, and, last, by S.S. Genovesi and Campi, so that it had the honor, which it still possesses, of being chosen by Emperors, Kings, Princes and Ambassadors, and by great men of all countries whose artistic travels bring them to this incomparable city, so justly called the « Pearl of the Adriatic ».

The delightful impression made on those who inhabit the Hotel Royal Danieli has been expressed over and over again to their friends, and they have often said to the proprietors that they have rather felt as if visiting in the house of a friend, or in a princely mansion, than in an hotel, even though in the greatest hotel in the world.

SANSOVINO HALL

In this lovely palace the traveler feels *at home*. All is artistic and poetical. No long passages, painted in imitation marble, cold and draughty, and dreary! No long endless tables and big red velvet divans, as in a cafe! No long rows of rooms in which the furniture is so much alike that you cannot tell if you are in your own room or someone else's! Here is nothing conventional, nothing that is to be seen everywhere—whether among the mountains of Switzerland or on the boulevards of Paris, and which makes the traveler's life monotonous wherever he may be. Here, on the contrary, he finds himself in an atmosphere of *home*, of comfort, and of suitability to his position, however exalted that may be, and one in keeping with his romantic surroundings.

This has been the aim of those who have directed the decorations of the Hotel Royal Danieli, and they are happy in the thought that they have succeeded to the satisfaction of the visitors.

To sum up. The Hotel Royal Danieli, now entirely restored and embellished from ground to roof and decorated by the best Venetian artists, arranged with all the most modern appliances for comfort, can offer the following conveniences for travelers:—

POST OFFICE.
RAILWAY OFFICE.
MONEY EXCHANGE AND BANKING OFFICE.
TWO LIFTS.
ELECTRIC LIGHT IN EVERY ROOM.
STEAM HEATERS.
BATHS AND DOUCHE BATHS ON EVERY FLOOR.
STEAM BOILERS FOR HOT WATER.
PRIVATE LAUNDRY.
COURT OF HONOR, OR ATRIUM.
READING-ROOMS.
WRITING-ROOM.
SMOKING-ROOM AND AMERICAN BAR.
PUBLIC DRAWING-ROOM.
LADIES' DRAWING-ROOM.
CONCERT HALL.
BALL ROOM.
MUSIC ROOM.
BILLIARD ROOM.
RESTAURANT, AT EVERY HOUR.
TABLE D'HOTE, AT SEPARATE TABLES, &c., &c.

STEPS AND RENAISSANCE VESTIBULE

HALL OF THE WINTER GARDENS

Table d'hote at separate tables, &c., &c., and all conducted according to the most modern systems of comfort and elegance.

Although the present proprietors, Messrs. Genovesi, Campi, Bozzi & Co., have spent a veritable fortune this year in restorations and embellishments, so as to render the Hotel Royal Danieli the most comfortable, the most artistic and the most aristocratic hotel in Europe, yet they have in nothing augmented the prices, but have retained those moderate rates which have helped to render the Hotel Danieli so famous.

Nota bene—The ancient Palazzo Dandolo, now Hotel Royal Danieli, and all its internal arrangements, deserves a special visit from travelers who are sojourning in Venice, and the proprietors will be most happy to show the palace to all interested in the sights of Venice, whether they are resident in the hotel or not.

www.ingramcontent.com/pod-product-compliance
Ingram Content Group UK Ltd.
Pitfield, Milton Keynes, MK11 3LW, UK
UKHW042153281224
453045UK00004B/371